IAN McALLISTER & NICHOLAS READ

THE SEAL GARDEN

ORCA BOOK PUBLISHERS

Library and Archives Canada Cataloguing in Publication

McAllister, Ian, 1969–, author, photographer
The seal garden / Ian McAllister, Nicholas Read.
(My Great Bear Rainforest)

Issued in print and electronic formats.
ISBN 978-1-4598-1267-3 (hardcover).—ISBN 978-1-4598-1268-0 (pdf).—
ISBN 978-1-4598-1269-7 (epub)

1. Marine mammals—British Columbia—Pacific Coast—Juvenile
literature. 2. Marine mammals—British Columbia—Great Bear
Rainforest—Juvenile literature. 3. Pacific Coast (B.C.)—Juvenile
literature. 4. Great Bear Rainforest (B.C.)—Juvenile literature.
5. Coastal ecology—British Columbia—Juvenile literature.
6. Rain forest ecology—British Columbia.

Juvenile literature. I. Read, Nicholas, 1956–, author. II. Title.
QL721.5.M7M33 2018   j599.5097111   C2017-904538-5
                          c2017-904539-3

Summary: This nonfiction picture book is illustrated with stunning
wildlife photographs and tells the story of harbor seals and other marine
mammals seeking refuge in a seal garden in the Great Bear Sea.

First published in the United States, 2018
Library of Congress Control Number: 2017940689

MIX
Paper from
responsible sources
FSC® C016245
www.fsc.org
FSC

*Orca Book Publishers is dedicated to preserving the environment and has
printed this book on Forest Stewardship Council® certified paper.*

Orca Book Publishers gratefully acknowledges the support for
its publishing programs provided by the following agencies:
the Government of Canada through the Canada Book Fund and the
Canada Council for the Arts, and the Province of British Columbia
through the BC Arts Council and the Book Publishing Tax Credit.

Cover and interior images by Ian McAllister
Edited by Sarah N. Harvey
Design by Rachel Page

About the photographs:
All of the images in this book are of wild animals in wild circumstances.
No digital manipulation or other alterations have taken place.

ORCA BOOK PUBLISHERS
www.orcabook.com

Printed and bound in Canada.

21 20 19 18 • 4 3 2 1

The storm is a big one. The wind whips the ocean waves into peaks as tall as trees. When storms like this happen in the Great Bear Sea, animals take cover.

In the forest, bears, deer and wolves duck under giant cedar trees that act like natural umbrellas. But out at sea, marine mammals seek a different kind of hiding place.

Seals, sea lions and otters take refuge from the worst of the storm in a magical place called a seal garden. Seal gardens are scattered throughout the Great Bear Sea and are arrangements of rocks that provide protection to many animals. It's a sanctuary from the punch of the waves and teeth of predators.

Seals, fish and smaller animals can get into the seal garden, but larger animals cannot.

Sometimes there are hundreds of marine mammals in a seal garden. They feed on the fish, bob like corks on the ocean's surface and wrap themselves in long copper-colored seaweed called kelp for afternoon naps.

Harbor **seals** *laze* in the middle of the seal garden while the much-larger California and Steller sea lions lounge on the outside rocks just above the pounding waves. Sea otters take shelter in the thick kelp forests too.

Harbor seals are about the size of a large man and are as cute as they are chubby. They have a thick layer of blubber that keeps them warm in the cold Pacific waters, and they come in many different colors. Some are even spotted like leopards. They are the most common seal in the ocean, and there are thousands of them in the Great Bear Sea.

Meanwhile, a giant northern elephant seal hauls its huge body out of the water for a rest. These enormous creatures can dive thousands of feet into the heart of the ocean in search of food. They are the second-biggest seals in the ocean. Only their cousins in the southern Pacific are larger.

Harbor seals aren't afraid of the storm because storms are so common in the Great Bear Sea. They know they just have to be patient while the storm blows itself out. Besides, the seal garden is the place to be in a storm because so many other seals are there too. It's a seal party.

Eventually the clouds disappear and the waves go flat. It's a perfect time for the seals to make their way out of the garden and into the open sea.

But when they do venture out to sea, the seals catch sight of the big black dorsal fins of three large orcas.

Fortunately, orcas are much too big to get into the seal garden. So as long as the seals turn around and head back to the garden before the orcas spy them, they will be safe.

Orcas like to sneak up on their prey, so the fact that the seals saw them first is bad news for the whales. Even so, once they spot the seals, they chase them all the way to the seal garden. They can see all the seals, sea lions, sea otters and river otters inside the garden, but they're too big to enter it.

The animals in the garden know the orcas can see them, because the shafts of sunlight cutting through the water act like spotlights. But there's nothing the orcas can do except hope that one of the animals inside the garden swims out of it into their hungry jaws. And that is unlikely.

Orcas are patient, and they patrol the garden like police. They hope to catch something, but even if they don't, they know that there are more gardens up the coast where they may have better luck.

Inside the garden, all the animals are nervous. Seals watch the orcas with wide eyes. Sea lions bark. River otters hide in rocky tunnels, and sea otters huddle in kelp beds. Meanwhile, the black fins keep circling and circling.

After an hour the orcas decide to move on, hoping to surprise the residents of the next seal garden up the coast.

That means the seals are safe. They can leave the seal garden to swim and fish and haul themselves out on rocks. The Great Bear Sea is a wonderful place to live, but it can be dangerous too. All the animals in the seal garden need to be smart and alert at all times. They need to know when it's safe to explore the Great Bear Sea and when it's wise to head back to the welcome haven of the seal garden.

It's the way of life in the Great Bear Sea,
where every animal, no matter how big or small,
has a place to live and a role to play.

Also in the *My Great Bear Rainforest* series

WOLF ISLAND

IAN McALLISTER & NICHOLAS READ

9781459812642 • $19.95 HC • Ages 5–8

"Enthralling fare for budding naturalists."

—*Kirkus Reviews for Wolf Island*

A BEAR'S LIFE

IAN McALLISTER & NICHOLAS READ

9781459812703 • $19.95 HC • Ages 5–8

"An appropriate companion to *Wolf Island* to nourish the sense of wonder."

—*Kirkus Reviews for A Bear's Life*

For more information about this spectacular place and Ian McAllister's stunning photography, please visit www.greatbearbooks.com or www.pacificwild.org.